REFLECT

THE BOLD JOURNAL

60 DAYS TO BECOME YOUR MOST VIBRANT, WEIRD, AND BOLD SELF

CASE KENNY

"I've changed so much I need to reintroduce myself"

THE BOLD JOURNAL

simple, intuitive journaling

10 minutes/day   *60 days of prompts*

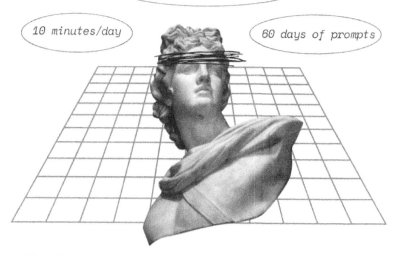

The Bold Journal is a 60-day guided journal to help you let go of who you're not so you can step into who you really are. A stronger you. A wiser you. A more unbothered you. A bolder you.

> To be bold is to find the magic of life that lives in the pages you turn, the new beginnings you embrace, the old chapters you leave behind, and the many reinventions along the way. To be bold is to no longer be subtle about what you want out of life.

About The Author

Case Kenny is an entrepreneur, mindfulness leader, host, and founder of the top 25 podcast "New Mindset, Who Dis" on both Apple Podcasts and Spotify. Beloved by some of today's biggest celebrities including Hailey Bieber, Sophia Bush, and Lucy Hale, Viola Davis, and featured on The Today Show and Good Morning America, you might recognize him from his viral coffee cup and post-it quotes on Instagram, which have been shared by millions and featured by The Today Show, Forbes, Fortune Magazine, Complex, Women's Health, Cosmopolitan, and many more.

Created in 2018, Kenny's podcast "New Mindset, Who Dis" features his short, no BS take on all things mindfulness in a relatable way - empowering people to be happier and live more fulfilling lives by changing their mindsets in all areas of life spanning from self-worth and empowerment to dating and relationships, career advice, and more.

Kenny also produces special "Music x Mindfulness" episodes where he collaborates with top artists and DJs including Martin Garrix, Gryffin, Cheat Codes, Sam Feldt, and others to bring mindfulness to life in an energizing and unique way for listeners.

For the latest, follow on Instagram @case.kenny.

Also available:

That's Bold of You: learn to thrive as your most vibrant, real, and weird self.

The New Mindset Journal: learn to love yourself again by gaining clarity on who you are and what you want in life.

But First, Inner Peace: discover how to create more, better, or different in your life.

Unbothered: unburden yourself of anxious thoughts and overthinking by finding your inner place of peace.

Single Is Your Superpower: discover exactly what you want (and deserve) in a partner and love yourself no matter what.

CLOSURE: become totally at peace with your past, your ex, or any relationship that drained you.

CLARITY: Answer the question, "Is it a YES or a NO?" with confidence and no overthinking.

To view books on Amazon scan below:

The beauty of life comes from your boldness.

That's making music or art simply because you want to. It's pursuing what makes you curious. It's replacing "maybe" with "definitely." It's listening to other people's stories, learning new cultures, and tasting new foods. It's introducing yourself to new people and realizing your dreams aren't as unrealistic as you once thought. It's opening your heart and letting new kinds of love in. It's being willing to change your mind. It's being present. It's being an occasional hot mess. It's moving at your own pace. It's striving to be whole, not perfect.

Life can be messy, but being bold is what makes it a beautiful mess.

Welcome to **The BOLD Journal**, a 60-day guided journal filled with prompts, quotes, meditations, and affirmations to help you let go of who you're not so you can step into who you really are.

One of the best compliments you can receive in life is: "Wow, you've changed." Your ability to change is the clearest proof you have that YOU are in charge of the direction of your life. We all need change - compassionate, honest, real, and progressive change. Sometimes it might be a small change like a new standard, boundary, or daily routine. Sometimes it might be a big change like ending a relationship, starting a new job, or moving cities - but change is a requirement of life. It's how you evolve. It's how you embrace who you are and leave behind who you are not.

Change is a reflection of lessons learned, forgiveness given, and hope that what lies ahead is better than your past. Change is believing in yourself again. It's reinventing yourself. It's recognizing that you know what it's like to just exist - unbold, uncurious, uninspired. You know what it's like to take a step back when everything inside of you wants you to step forward. That is why it's time to be bold. That is your why. That is your fire.

The boldest thing we can do in life is to see yourself through your own eyes again. It's to create your own version of too much and take back control of the labels that you've let become your identity. It's to give yourself credit for who you really are and just let people see you through the lens of their own reality. If they misunderstand you or want a different version of you, that's okay, but you're no longer negotiating your self-judgment.

This is a journal to help you reinvent yourself. It's a journal to help you become who you're supposed to be and let go of who you're not in the process. It's a journal that will leave you saying to yourself, "I've changed so much I need to reintroduce myself."

To be bold is to give yourself permission to be rooted in the present moment.

Easier said than done, right? No matter where you are in life, there is ALWAYS something distracting you. Rushing you. Pressuring you. We're all under a lot of pressure to have it ALL figured out right now. We're pressured to have a 5, 10, or 20-year plan. We're pressured to have our relationships, health, habits, finances, and friendships figured out right now. We're pressured to think that everyone else has life all figured out and we need to keep up with them. The result? We rush. We accept good enough. We compare ourselves from a place of lack. We grab onto the first thing that makes sense and turn our backs on more, better, different, or simpler.

That pressure and the resistance to change that comes from it doesn't open us up to reinvention. It leads us to stick out a static path because it's "what we were told to do," it's safe or realistic, or we don't want to start over. Those beliefs make us stagnant and rob us of possibility. They don't open us up to the magic of life - which lives in the pages we turn, the new chapters we start, the old chapters we leave behind, and the many reinventions along the way.

This journal is designed to unburden you of pressure to have it all figured out, and instead, bring you back to the present.

You don't have to have it all figured out right now. All you have to figure out is right now.

For the next 60 days, you're going to let go of pressure. You're going to let go of judgment. You're going to let go of "supposed to be." You're going to focus on today, because in the present, you find your true self. And once you find clarity there, the rest comes together like pieces of a puzzle finding their rightful positions.

The question you're going to ask yourself on a daily basis is: what makes me feel most like myself? In this moment, in this chapter, and at this point in my life, what makes me feel most like myself? What job makes me feel most like myself? What partner makes me feel most like myself? What city? What wellness routine? What friend group? What music? What books?

What makes you feel like yourself? That is the question.

Spend time answering this question, and you'll find the magic of life that exists in the present. That's the gift of waking up each day with freedom of choice and freedom of intention. By answering this question, you empower yourself to change - if you invested time into being a certain way or working a certain job because at one point it made you feel most like yourself, but then you realized you're called to something else, that is a gift. When you decide to change, it doesn't mean you're falling behind, it doesn't mean you're the only one without a master plan... it's the opposite. When you're willing to embrace change, you're moving close to figuring it all out. You're saying, "In this moment, I feel most like myself and I'm acting on it."

Change doesn't mean you're moving further away from the life you deserve; it means you're moving closer to it.

It's our job in life to find moments that make us feel most like ourselves. It's our job to examine ourselves honestly, compassionately, and vulnerably, and to say: does this make me feel most like myself? Am I challenging myself to be able to tell? And then along the way, you collect those moments, those experiences, and you make a vision from it. You don't have to have it all figured out right now. Hold yourself accountable, don't get too comfortable, don't accept good enough, but take the pressure off to have it all figured out. Just figure out right now.

Ask yourself, in this moment, in this city, with my habit, this job, this relationship status, do I feel most like myself? Yes? Keep exploring that. No? Make a change. A big one or a small one - whatever your responsibilities, financial situation, and health permits.

Whatever you do, please don't think you're falling behind when you don't know for sure where these moments will lead you or what the 5, 10-year plan is. That is the gift of life - to continue to collect moments that matter, to savor them, and to use them to continue to roll out the road ahead... mile by mile, exit by exit, step by step, and chapter by chapter.

You don't have to have it all figured out right now.
You just have to figure out right now.

To be bold is to let people lose you
instead of begging them to choose you.

To be bold is to stop allowing
anyone to save you for later.

To be bold is to do things simply
because they bring you joy.

To be bold is to delete their number
and welcome new energy into your life.

To be bold is to realize you're not everyone's
cup of tea... and you're fine with it.

To be bold is to prioritize slow
mornings, good books, and inner peace.

To be bold is to give yourself the same
love you always gave others.

To be bold is to decide your honesty doesn't
make you "too much" or an inconvenience.

To be bold is to decide you deserve more
than someone who is unsure about you.

To be bold is to stop minimizing
yourself to please certain people.

Instructions

This journal values simplicity and pressure-free honesty over everything else. Journaling shouldn't make you feel overwhelmed with prompts, pressured to complete a checklist by a certain time each day, or left feeling confused or anxious. **The Bold Journal** offers the simplest and most impactful form of journaling with a mix of daily peace and energy. Each day consists of the following:

- a quote/affirmation
- x2 check-in journal prompts
- x1 in-depth question

Each day should take 10-15 minutes and can be done at any time. Don't feel pressured to do it in the morning if you have a busy day. Don't feel pressured to do it at night if you're feeling exhausted. Complete your daily prompts when you have time and when you're in the right headspace. If you feel like you're forcing answers or you're feeling resistant to being honest, take a day off and come back. Feel free to write in complete sentences or shorthand - whatever works best for you to get your thoughts out. It doesn't have to be pretty, poetic, or look good for other people. Your answers are YOUR answers.

Every three days, you'll be presented with a perspective to consider. These offer simple and short mindsets that can inspire change. Feel free to mark them up, highlight, draw, or circle any words or thoughts that speak to you.

- be present: a fundamental requirement to making your journaling experience real and honest is presence. Bring your mind and body to the same place. Be in the moment. It's only for 10-15 minutes. Put your phone away and tune out distractions.

- **mix up where you journal:** try different settings. Some people respond best to utter silence, others to a busy coffee shop, a park bench, or somewhere else. Experiment.

- **get in the right headspace:** if you find yourself struggling to find your "honesty switch," try listening to music. The right music can get you in a flow state where your honesty comes easier. We love dance music for its progressive, uplifting, and melodic structure.

- **be honest:** push yourself to be vulnerable and don't just write what "sounds good." Journaling is about affirming what you know to be true but also about being honest about what you don't know, what frustrates you, what makes you feel anxious, and what you need to do despite how difficult it might be. It's ok if you find yourself writing similar answers on multiple days - that means you're finding a pattern. Good!

- **don't be gentle:** to get the journal to lay flat while you journal, fold the pages aggressively on a flat surface :)

This journal pairs well with:

- *That's Bold of You* - a mindful guide to becoming your realest and most vibrant self (available on Amazon).

- The *New Mindset, Who Dis* **podcast** – short episodes with no BS, simple mindfulness released twice a week. (to listen on Apple Podcasts, scan below)

To be bold is to stop saying "sorry"
and just let yourself take up space.

To be bold is to stop keeping
tabs on the people you've outgrown.

To be bold is to stop letting
social media rush you through life.

To be bold is to stop saying
"yes" when you want to say "no."

To be bold is to decide you still have
time to do everything you want in life.

To be bold is to prioritize how
your life feels instead of how it looks.

To be bold is to decide your past
mistakes don't make you any less lovable.

To be bold is to let go of "supposed to be"
timing and just trust in your own.

To be bold is to no longer be subtle
about what and who you want.

To be bold is to start believing in yourself
like you always believe in others.

Dedicate the next 60 days to embracing what makes you, you. Too loud. Too quiet. Too difficult. Too much. Too bold. Too cringe.

Sometimes the world doesn't know what to do with people like you. It will try to put you in a box of expectations. It will try to keep you on pace with "supposed to be" timelines. But how could that path be meant for someone like you?

Your ambition can light up an entire city. Your heart can carry the weight of the world's troubles, but you still believe in goodness. You lend a hand even when your own are full. You see hope where others see despair. You're not afraid to be wildly different. You care more about how your life feels to YOU than how it looks to other people.

How could you be meant for "supposed to be?" Don't let anyone convince you to diminish your fire to blend into their world. The people who say you're "cringe" are the same people who would rather disappoint themselves than disappoint others. They're the same people who would rather shrink themselves down and get a favorable label of "cool" or "normal" than step into a version of life that actually delivers what they want.

You're not them. The next 60 days are dedicated to letting go of the part of you that cringes, not the part of you that is cringe. That is your superpower. That is what will set you free.

Let's get started.

Day 1/60

****

I'd rather be a hot mess
of happiness than perfect.

I don't need to keep up with
everyone else to be happy.

I don't need to be everyone's
cup of tea to be happy.

I don't need to have it all
figured out to be happy.

One thing I have:

One thing I want:

I'm the kind of person who:

On the below graph, create a visual representation of your happiness over the years. For the peaks and valleys, add a note about what you were doing when you were happy/unhappy/in-between.

H
A
P
P
I
N
E
S
S

BORN   PRESENT DAY

****

The best revenge is no revenge.

It's to become the person no one
thought you were capable of becoming.
It's to decide someone else's ceiling in
life is not your own. It's to move on
and let karma sort out the rest.

It's to have the audacity to give
yourself what someone else wouldn't.

REFLECT: one word to describe how you currently feel:

REINVENT: one word to describe how you want to feel:

REBEL: one thing you can do today that is the opposite of what you've been doing:

If I prioritized how my life looks to other people, I would:

If I prioritized how my life feels to me, I would:

In what areas of your life do you NOT feel like yourself?
What is the cause of not feeling like yourself? Is it other
people? A job? A habit? Where do you still feel like you're
"faking it" and why?

****

May you attract people in your life
who are good for your soul - who
see your scars as part of your story,
not something to be fixed.

They don't fumble what you bring
to the table. They see your magic
and help you spread it.

What's the best that could happen in your life right now?

One thing I can control:

One thing I should accept:

How do you deserve to be treated by the people in your life - friends, family, coworkers, and romantic partners? Why do you deserve those things? Be specific about reciprocity (i.e., you offer certain things, so you deserve to receive them in return):

Why should you be bold?

If you're reading this, you have a beautiful heart, kind energy, a powerful voice, passion, and pizazz for a reason. It's time to shine your light, speak your mind, and embrace your own label of being "too much." It's time to be bold.

You should step into this bolder version of yourself because you know what it's like to NOT be bold.

You know what it's like to tiptoe around people, trying to be everyone's cup of tea, and where "sorry" is the most common word out of your mouth. You know what it's like to change your wants, needs, or behavior to make sure everyone around you is comfortable. You know what it's like to succumb to advice, timelines, or definitions that are "realistic."

You know what it's like to make yourself small in the face of your big goals and aspirations. You know what it's like to stick it out in relationships that no longer serve you. You know what it's like to let other people have the spotlight. You know what it's like to take a step back when everything inside of you wants you to step forward.

Being bold doesn't mean you're full of yourself. It doesn't mean you're the loudest person in the room. It doesn't mean you're perfect. It simply means you embrace the "beautiful mess" of your life in everything you do.

It means you realize that life can be messy but being "too much" is what makes it a beautiful mess.

****

You have a beautiful heart,
kind energy, a powerful
voice, passion, and pizazz
for a reason.

You're exactly who
you're supposed to be.

I deserve:

because I:

One thing I'm looking forward to:

Complete the following sentence with as many "I" statements as possible:

*I love myself most when*_____.

Describe the specific feelings, activities, or circumstances that make you feel in love with yourself:

Day 5/60

****

When you're willing to love fully
and without limits... you don't lose
anybody, they lose you.

When you show up as the most
vibrant and real version of yourself...
you don't lose anybody, they lose you.

When you have a weird sense of humor, a
kind soul, and offer unquestionable loyalty...
you don't lose anybody, they lose you.

I don't ever want to look back and regret:

What's bothering you/on your mind right now?

One thing you will NEVER accept, tolerate, or settle for:

What have you tolerated from people in the past that you refuse to accept now? What happened in your life that changed your mind? Remind yourself what you will not tolerate from others by completing the following as many times as you can: *I will no longer tolerate* _____

Day 6/60

You're not missing out when
you decide how your life FEELS
to you is more important than
how it LOOKS to others.

One thing I have:

One thing I want:

I'm the kind of person who:

Is there anything you're trying to prove to others right now? Does it come from a healthy and fair place or is it borrowed and unfair to you? Why are you trying to prove this thing? Is it different from what you're trying to prove to yourself?

The most attractive thing about you...

The most attractive thing about you is your ability to NOT become what has happened to you.

It's attractive to experience things in life that objectively suck but to NOT turn around and become those things yourself. I know that sounds idealistic, but I can't think of a more attractive quality than to be so radically and stubbornly rooted in love that you refuse to allow anyone, any circumstance, or any past experience to rob you of your hope and goodness.

The most attractive thing about you is:

- to compliment others even when no one is complimenting you.

- to listen even when no one else is listening to you.

- if you've been ghosted or cheated on...you don't do the same.

- to be optimistic when everyone around you is anything but.

- to be compassionate and caring even when everyone else says to be selfish or savage.

What a powerfully attractive quality! That's to have experienced people and events in life that didn't recognize your worth but to not turn cold, and to not turn around and treat others in the same way.

The most attractive thing about you is your ability to not become what has happened to you. It's to love yourself so much that that hope radiates to the world around you.... because you refuse to let anyone rob you of it. That is attractive.

****

You know you're on the right track
when you're grateful for not getting
what you once wanted because now
you know you deserve better.

You care more about quality than
quantity in all areas of your life.

You appreciate what you had
without needing to go back to it.

You'd rather be "too much" than
apologize for being yourself.

You're on the right track.

REFLECT: one word to describe how you currently feel:

REINVENT: one word to describe how you want to feel:

REBEL: one thing you can do today that is the opposite of what you've been doing:

If I prioritized how my life looks to other people, I would:

If I prioritized how my life feels to me, I would:

Envision your "boldest self" - what are three things that version of yourself would be doing right now that you're not currently doing? Why aren't you doing those things? What is holding you back?

Day 8/60

****

Your younger self would be proud of you
for creating a life that's right for YOU - not
your parents, the internet, or a checklist.

That's a life where you become your own
source of happiness. You prioritize liking
yourself over being liked by everyone.
You show up as the real you even when
it's easier to water yourself down.

What's the best that could happen in your life right now?

One thing I can control:

One thing I should accept:

What are three things you want to be remembered for? Why do you want those things to be your legacy?

****

If you're seeing this, there's a
few things you should know:

The world needs your weirdness,
thoughtfulness, and smile.

You deserve to be loved even if
you're still learning to love yourself.

It's your turn to have the spotlight
you've always given to others.

You're about to break through
whatever is holding you back.

You're a total catch.

I deserve:

because I:

One thing I'm looking forward to:

In 2-3 sentences, describe version 1.0 of yourself (who you used to be).

In 2-3 sentences, describe version 2.0 of yourself (who you're becoming... your boldest self).

The most important decision you'll ever make...

What do you think the most important decision you'll ever make is? Is it who you date? Where you live? How many children you have? How you invest your money?

Those are very important decisions, but there's an even more important one, and it's a mindset decision. That decision is:

Is the world FOR you or AGAINST you?

This decision is predicated on the fact that the assumptions you make about life create your reality and your actions follow suit. If the world is against you, if life is unfair, if everyone is dishonest, if you're an unlucky person... you don't try, you don't open yourself to love, you don't shoot your shot, you close off. You accept what you can get. You take whatever love, passion, or connection is available.

But if the world is for you... you have confidence in the DIRECTION of your life. You believe in possibility, goodness, and connection. You apply for that job, you start that business, you make that investment. You believe in your ability to either succeed OR rebound if you don't.

This ONE assumption dictates EVERYTHING. It dictates what you accept. Your standards. Your aspirations. Your expectations of what is possible.

Is the world for you or against you?

Day 10/60

Think about how far you've come
in life and what you've overcome
getting to this point.

You didn't come this far to be
subtle about what you want. You
didn't come this far to think you're
only worthy of being half-loved.
You didn't come this far to feel
guilty for asking for more.

You didn't come this far to let anyone
talk you out of what you deserve.

I don't ever want to look back and regret:

What's bothering you/on your mind right now?

One thing you will NEVER accept, tolerate, or settle for:

What's missing in your life right now? A person? An experience? An achievement? What would having that thing offer you on an inner level? How would it enhance or change your life for the better? How would it bring out the boldest version of yourself?

Day 11/60

Your best days are
not behind you.

You have not seen it all.
You have not felt it all.

There are more places for
you to see, people to meet,
and firsts to experience.

One thing I have:

One thing I want:

I'm the kind of person who:

Make a list of five places in the world you'd like to visit. Be specific and include what you'd like to do in each place and how the experience there would make you feel:

Day 12/60

Affirm:

Soon I will see that the universe has
been conspiring in my favor all along.

Soon I will meet the proof that my
standards were never too high.

Soon I will win the battle with the
thing I don't tell anyone about.

Soon I will start a new chapter
which proves every setback was
a setup for something better.

REFLECT: one word to describe how you currently feel:

REINVENT: one word to describe how you want to feel:

REBEL: one thing you can do today that is the opposite of what you've been doing:

If I prioritized how my life looks to other people, I would:

If I prioritized how my life feels to me, I would:

What is something you want to experience again in life, but this time what will be different about it? What did you learn the first time that fuels this change? How would it feel to have this new experience?

What if you're wrong?

Limiting beliefs...

"I'm not smart enough, attractive enough, funny enough, whatever enough."

Those are beliefs that hold you back from trying - from applying to that job, talking to that person, starting that passion project, getting off the couch and dating, etc.

Something I do that really helps me ACT despite those feelings is I ask myself: "What if I'm wrong? What if I've backed myself into a corner for no reason? Do I have definitive proof in my life that my assumptions are true? Do I have proof that I am indeed not smart enough, not talented enough, or not worthy enough, etc.?"

Probably not. What about you? If you're wrong, wouldn't it change things? And it begs the question: if you're wrong... then why not you?

In a world where someone is going to WIN - someone is going to be happy and fulfilled in their career, someone is going to travel the world and experience everything they dream of, someone is going to find their person and they're going to live an incredible life together, someone is going to ask for what they want and they're going to get it - why can't that person be you?

Why? Not? You?

Create a window of opportunity for yourself to prove that your limiting beliefs are WRONG. Ask yourself that question, realize you likely don't have proof... and then act.

What if you're wrong? Why not you?

****

I'm better off being disappointed
by the things I tried and failed than
regretting the chances I never took.
I'm better off starting over than sticking
out something that no longer serves me.
I'm better off being unapologetically
"too much" than apologizing for
being myself.

- note to self

What's the best that could happen in your life right now?

One thing I can control:

One thing I should accept:

What's something you tried and failed in the past? How did it feel to fail? What did you learn? What are the promises you can make yourself as a result of what you learned? Write out as many promises as you can from past failures.

"I promise myself _____"

Day 14/60

Inner peace is luxury.

That's taking your own advice and
finally deciding you deserve better. It's
making yourself unavailable to anyone
who treats you like an option. It's respecting
your intuition. It's staying in your own
lane and creating your own path.

I deserve:

because I:

One thing I'm looking forward to:

What are FIVE things you love about yourself? Be specific and write each out:

"I love that I _____."

****

Real closure is not wanting to change
the past because you're stronger as
a result. It's turning a disappointing
story into a higher standard. It's being
OK with unfinished endings, messy
conclusions, and words left unsaid.

Real closure is deciding your next
chapter is going to be your best yet.

I don't ever want to look back and regret:

What's bothering you/on your mind right now?

One thing you will NEVER accept, tolerate, or settle for:

What has been the greatest personal change you've ever made that looking back on it, makes you proud? Was it a change to your habits? A career change? A relationship change? Describe the change itself and how it has enhanced your life:

Take a step back

Are you too close to see the answer? Is there something you're so close to in life that you don't see the way out, the thing you should do, or maybe a more compassionate way to feel?

This might help. I saw a thread on Reddit where someone asked: what is the most helpful thing your therapist has ever said to you? Here was someone's answer:

"My therapist and I were discussing how I felt about a pretty deep betrayal from my now ex-wife. I was beating myself up for not seeing how bad she really was when there was plenty of evidence.

My therapist wrote down something on his yellow notepad and then held it up right in my face, practically touching my nose. He said, "What's that say?" I couldn't read it; it was too close to my face. Stepping back from it a bit, I could read that it said, "You're too close to see it." He was right.

I was too close to the problems and the situation to have been able to see it, where in retrospect, it was so obvious. I stopped beating myself up over it and was able to let it go."

Think about that thing that's on your mind that you can't escape or find clarity on. Take a step back. Maybe you're too close? Try asking yourself: if a friend were to ask you what to do, what would you say?

Sometimes clarity presents itself when you find a way to observe instead of feel, and in this case, the question: "If a friend were to ask you what to do," might be just the thing you need to take a step back.

Day 16/60

Life isn't about being perfect.
It's about being so ridiculously
passionate that people think
you're a little crazy.

One thing I have:

One thing I want:

I'm the kind of person who:

Complete this sentence 5 times:

"*I am worthy of a peaceful life because* _____."

Be specific and give yourself credit for all the things you do, your effort, and your commitment.

I am worthy of a peaceful life because

I am worthy of a peaceful life because

I am worthy of a peaceful life because

I am worthy of a peaceful life because

I am worthy of a peaceful life because

Day 17/60

The happiest people are too busy
doing their own thing to compare
themselves to others.

REFLECT: one word to describe how you currently feel:

REINVENT: one word to describe how you want to feel:

REBEL: one thing you can do today that is the opposite of what you've been doing:

If I prioritized how my life looks to other people, I would:

If I prioritized how my life feels to me, I would:

What traits do you admire in other people? Why? Do you admire the same traits in yourself? Are you working on those traits in yourself? What's stopping you? Be specific about the traits you admire and what stepping into them yourself would offer you in your life:

Day 18/60

Some people will
misunderstand you.

Sometimes your big heart
will be too much for others.

But you have a unique
combination of mind,
body, and soul. You have
depth. Intuition. Empathy.

How could you be
meant for everyone?

What's the best that could happen in your life right now?

One thing I can control:

One thing I should accept:

In what areas of your life do you over-care what others think about you? Why do you think that is? Why are you putting so much emphasis on other people's opinions?

If you feel like you're falling behind...

One of the most helpful responses I've heard to the question: "What's your best piece of life wisdom?" came from someone in their 70s and is as follows.

"What seems like a big deal now, isn't–no matter your age. When you're 33, you're not gonna care about your unrequited crush, though your 15-year-old mind can't fathom it.

When you're 50, you won't stress about costing your company an important client, though your 33-year-old mind thinks you've permanently destroyed your career.

When you're 70, it won't matter that the house you bought at 50 wasn't the good investment you'd hoped.

Don't stress yourself out because most of today's earth-shattering events are tomorrow's inconsequential BS."

I don't have all the answers, and yes, some life events are permanent, but we'll never know in the present. We're always rushing in life - both literally in thinking we're out of time and figuratively with the negative assumptions we make. That worrying and rushing makes us suffer twice or as Seneca says: "We suffer more in imagination than we do in reality."

I talk to people in their 20s and they feel like they're falling behind, that they're out of time, and I talk to people in their 60s and they say they're just getting started. The difference is perspective and trust.

All we can do is move forward with the mentality of the saying: "You can't connect the dots looking forward; you can only connect them looking backwards." We have to trust that the dots will connect in the future and in the meanwhile, we make the most of the time we've been given.

Day 19/60

The question isn't: "What if I'm falling behind?"
But rather: "What if I'm just building something better?"

The question isn't: "What if I'm being selfish?"
But rather :"What if I'm just finally respecting myself?"

The question isn't: "What if my best days are behind me?"
But rather: "What if I'm just getting started?"

I deserve:

because I:

One thing I'm looking forward to:

What are three "what if" questions on your mind right now?
Write each down.

"What if_____?"

How would it feel to be able to answer each question? Are
there any small steps today you can take to find clarity?

Day 20/60

You are so much more
than the times you thought
your softness was a weakness.

You are so much more
than the people who used you
while they figured out what they wanted.

You are so much more
than the times you thought
you needed to prove you're lovable.

I don't ever want to look back and regret:

What's bothering you/on your mind right now?

One thing you will NEVER accept, tolerate, or settle for:

What do you know to be true about life today that you didn't know a year ago? Complete this sentence three times:

I'm at the age where _____

I'm at the age where _____

I'm at the age where _____

****

Forgiveness.

I forgive myself for all the times
I didn't think I was good enough,
smart enough, or worthy enough.

I forgive myself for looking for
love in the same places I lost it.

I forgive myself for thinking I had
to convince someone to love me
in the same way I loved them.

I forgive myself for not asking for
more when I knew I deserved it.

It's a new day.

One thing I have:

One thing I want:

I'm the kind of person who:

Is there anything you need to forgive yourself for right now? Why haven't you forgiven yourself yet? What would self-forgiveness offer you? Write it three times:

I forgive myself for _____

I forgive myself for _____

I forgive myself for _____

If you're struggling to forgive yourself...

What are you hesitant to forgive yourself for?

- Believing in potential with your ex?

- Trying and failing at that business?

- Not standing up for yourself, not asking for more, going back to someone when you shouldn't have?

Those are common things that we tend to hang onto, and we resist forgiving ourselves for. But what do all those things have in common? Those were all moments where you trusted yourself. You trusted that compatibility was there with your ex. You trusted you had what it takes to try that business. You trusted that not speaking up, playing it cool, matching energy, going back to that person... was the right decision for YOU.

In that moment, you trusted yourself and you acted thinking it was the right move. Now with hindsight, you realize it wasn't, but without much thinking, we carry around this guilt and this shame of having gotten something wrong. Let's hit reset. We can hang onto weight like that forever if we hold ourselves to a standard of always needing to get things right in life - and if that's the case... it's no wonder it's tough to forgive yourself. When you're struggling to forgive yourself, you're really struggling to trust yourself again. Can you give yourself another shot at trusting yourself?

That is forgiveness. You deserve to trust that your empathy is always well-served. You deserve to trust that your inclination to see the best in others is always well-served. Forgiving yourself means trusting yourself again, and you deserve to trust yourself.

Day 22/60

There's something beautiful about YOU.

You choose inner peace over "people pleasing." You don't put your value in the hands of other people. You aren't interested in fitting inside the mold of what's expected of you. You refuse to let what broke you follow you any further.

Beautiful.

REFLECT: one word to describe how you currently feel:

REINVENT: one word to describe how you want to feel:

REBEL: one thing you can do today that is the opposite of what you've been doing:

If I prioritized how my life looks to other people, I would:

If I prioritized how my life feels to me, I would:

The best revenge is to have the audacity to give yourself what they wouldn't. What are three things you can give yourself right now? What are three things that no one can take from you once you decide to give them to yourself?

Day 23/60

Just so we're clear, I'm not interested
in being nonchalant. I want to be real.

I'm not here to be anyone's second choice.

If it's forced or fake, it's not for me.

My inner peace is more important
than anyone's approval.

- note to self

What's the best that could happen in your life right now?

One thing I can control:

One thing I should accept:

What's something you used to doubt about yourself but then you showed up and proved otherwise? How did it feel to silence that self-doubt? How can you prove your self-doubt wrong more often?

Day 24/60

Stay close to people who are
good for your mental health.

People who offer you new memories,
shared laughter, and matching energy.
People who know you're too fabulous
to be treated like an option. People who
understand you even when you're not
saying a single word. People who ask
how your day was AND want to read
your essay about it.

I deserve:

because I:

One thing I'm looking forward to:

Describe the kind of people you want in your life. List as many attributes as you can.

"I want to be surrounded by people who _____ *"*

Be specific about their behavior and how it makes you feel:

Do they deserve your energy?

It's ok to not care about or react to some things in life. If you're always listening, always reacting, and always giving emotional responses to everything... it's exhausting. It's OK to simply say, "This is not worth my energy."

Someone cuts you off in traffic... energy.
Someone is 15 minutes late to a zoom meeting... energy.
Someone is rude to you... energy.

Not everything deserves a reaction in life. This is an idea that comes from Marcus Aurelius and Meditations 6.52 which says, "It is in our power to have no opinion about a thing, and not to be disturbed in our soul; for things themselves have no natural power to form our judgments."

I'm drawn to this idea of Marcus Aurelius and the technique in philosophy called "Epoché." It's Greek, and it's a technical term typically translated as "suspension of judgment." Epoché. When something happens... you don't give it anything. You don't label it. You don't rationalize it. You just accept it as it is.

You've grown so much, you practice so much healthy and compassionate self-control in your life, you don't lower your standards for less than what you deserve, you put in hours and hours working your tail off, you love yourself, you love others. You're in the driver's seat... finally! But then in an instant, you surrender yourself to the little things. You let THEM draw emotion from you.

Does it deserve anything further? Does it deserve any further judgment? Do you need to hang onto this? Think about how peaceful it is to just observe life. That's power. That's self-control. That's boldness.

Day 25/60

Amidst everything life throws your way,
maybe there's still magic to appreciate?
Maybe it exists somewhere in-between the
uncertainty of the economy, the overwhelm
of the daily news cycle, or the angst that comes
from the latest "unprecedented times." Maybe
it exists where you decide to notice it?

Maybe it exists in the satisfaction of completing a
puzzle or crossword. Or nailing the high notes when
it's your turn at karaoke. Or finding solace in a book.
Or biting into a perfectly ripe piece of fruit. Or eye
contact and a smile from a stranger. Or finding an
extra fry at the bottom of the bag.

Maybe it exists in the simple moments all around
you. Someone singing along to a song while sitting
in traffic. A random act of kindness. A dog happily
wagging its tail. A farmer's market brimming with
colorful produce. The sounds of birds chirping and
the rustling of leaves in a park. The comforting ambiance
of clinking cups and plates coming from a restaurant.
A stranger offering up their seat on the train. Magic.

I don't ever want to look back and regret:

What's bothering you/on your mind right now?

One thing you will NEVER accept, tolerate, or settle for:

What's a positive feeling you once felt and never want to forget? Take yourself back to that feeling and describe how it came about. How can you put yourself in a position to feel that way again?

Day 26/60

Life gets better when:

you decide the bare minimum you've
been offered is not what you deserve.

you realize your worth is not determined
by one person's inability to see it.

you decide you don't need anyone's approval
or permission to do what's best for you.

you'd rather hear NO and have a
story to tell than no story at all.

One thing I have:

One thing I want:

I'm the kind of person who:

What is a question you wished someone would ask you more often? What would your answer to the question be? How would it feel to have a conversation with someone else about this?

Day 27/60

I'm grateful for not being everyone's
cup of tea - it made me realize I'm my
own cup of tea and that's all that matters.

REFLECT: one word to describe how you currently feel:

REINVENT: one word to describe how you want to feel:

REBEL: one thing you can do today that is the opposite of what you've been doing:

If I prioritized how my life looks to other people, I would:

If I prioritized how my life feels to me, I would:

What's something you're avoiding in your life right now?
Why? What would it take to move forward in a small way?
What would progress in this area offer you on an inner level?

That mind though...

Your mind is what makes you unique. Without my mind, what am I? I'm literally just a body. Just a sack of potatoes. Your attraction to others is the way they think... it's the way they see the world, the things that come from their mind - the sense of adventure, sense of humor, values, morals, etc.

What greater gift is there than to see the world through the lens of your mind? Our minds are what makes us, us. The way we react to the world around us is what makes us, us. We need to be proud of ourselves and how we think - no matter if we're prone to overthinking, no matter if we're prone to being socially anxious, too introverted, or too extroverted, etc.

Your "too much" is someone's version of perfect.

Your sense of adventure and spontaneity is someone's version of perfect.

Your laugh and sense of humor is someone's version of perfect.

Your eagerness and oversharing is someone's version of perfect.

Your mind is what makes you, you, and with enough time, we all eventually come back to the truth that it's something to celebrate, not a detractor from our life's happiness. It's the source of your kindness, your curiosity, your realness, and your courage. Can we take a step back and appreciate what makes us, us? Can we appreciate our minds in the same way we appreciate others? You're never missing out when you lead with what's in your mind. You're never missing out when you tap into the kindness, the curiosity, the realness that sits in your head.

Day 28/60

****

The world belongs to the
soulful wanderers who don't
know exactly where they're going
but always end up where they belong.

What's the best that could happen in your life right now?

One thing I can control:

One thing I should accept:

Make a list of simple pleasures that bring you joy. Next to each simple pleasure, write how it makes you feel:

Day 29/60

The next part of your life
begins when you decide:

you're done being subtle
about what and who you want

you're no longer willing
to accept "good enough"

you decide to give yourself the
same love you always give others

I deserve:

because I:

One thing I'm looking forward to:

What would you do right now if you couldn't fail? What is the immediate next step you'd take? How would doing this thing make you feel?

Day 30/60

The power of NO.

It's gonna be a NO from me if
you treat me like a side dish.

It's gonna be a NO from me if
you only want me on your terms.

It's gonna be a NO from me if
you bring unnecessary drama into my life.

It's gonna be a NO from me if
you don't amplify the happiness
I've worked so hard to create.

I don't ever want to look back and regret:

What's bothering you/on your mind right now?

One thing you will NEVER accept, tolerate, or settle for:

What triggers you in life? Do you notice any patterns with those triggers? Do certain people or contexts bring them out in you more than others?

How to be present

We owe it to ourselves to be present in our life's experiences as we live them - not in retrospect, not looking back and saying, "Those WERE good times, those WERE the days, or that WAS such a special moment."

These ARE the good times, these ARE the days, and these ARE the special moments.

Ask yourself this: "What is something in my life that I want to go back and experience for the first time again?" There's something special about "firsts" in life. But we really only tend to realize this by looking back.

We can make a decision that literally everything we do in the present can be approached with enthusiasm as if it were a first. Pretend you're living a "first" today.

The past isn't here with us anymore and the future hasn't happened yet... and we're giving all of our living energy to those things?! Yes, it's great to look back and learn from your past. Yes, it's great to work to create the life you want in the future. But we need to carve out time today to be in today.

Approach this day as a special time in your life. A Tuesday at 11:00 AM. A Friday out with friends. A coffee. A meal. Chipotle.

Pretend it's for the first time again. And remember what it's like to experience something for the first time KNOWING that in retrospect, it's a special moment. Be in the moment. Soak up the details. Listen to that song and just appreciate it. Taste the coffee. Shake their hands with enthusiasm. Make eye contact first.

What if you approached today as if it's for the first time?

Day 31/60

Why are you afraid to start
over when every time you have,
you've come back stronger,
smarter, and more attractive?

One thing I have:

One thing I want:

I'm the kind of person who:

What is something you say but don't actually do? What advice do you know you should take but rarely do? Be honest about your hesitancy to take your own advice:

****

You're not missing out when:

you refuse to let someone
save you for later.

you prioritize liking yourself
over being liked by everyone.

you walk away from anyone who
treats you like a backup plan.

you decide you'd rather be alone
than lonely with someone else.

REFLECT: one word to describe how you currently feel:

```
┌─────────────────────────────────────────────┐
│                                             │
│                                             │
│                                             │
└─────────────────────────────────────────────┘
```

REINVENT: one word to describe how you want to feel:

```
┌─────────────────────────────────────────────┐
│                                             │
│                                             │
│                                             │
└─────────────────────────────────────────────┘
```

REBEL: one thing you can do today that is the opposite of what you've been doing:

```
┌─────────────────────────────────────────────┐
│                                             │
│                                             │
│                                             │
│                                             │
└─────────────────────────────────────────────┘
```

If I prioritized how my life looks to other people, I would:

```
┌─────────────────────────────────────────────┐
│                                             │
│                                             │
│                                             │
│                                             │
│                                             │
│                                             │
│                                             │
└─────────────────────────────────────────────┘
```

If I prioritized how my life feels to me, I would:

```
┌─────────────────────────────────────────────┐
│                                             │
│                                             │
│                                             │
│                                             │
│                                             │
│                                             │
│                                             │
└─────────────────────────────────────────────┘
```

What's one thing you think is overrated in life? What's one thing you think is underrated?

Day 33/60

Gratitude.

I'm grateful for the times I didn't end up with what I thought I wanted... because now I know I deserve better.

I'm grateful for the times I asked for more and was told no... because it made me even more ambitious.

I'm grateful for the times I moved on without the apology I deserved... because now I know I can create my own closure.

I'm grateful for people who said I was "too much"... because they showed me that some people aren't enough for ME.

What's the best that could happen in your life right now?

One thing I can control:

One thing I should accept:

Look around you. What are five things you're grateful for right now?

Does time heal all wounds?

Practically I think the saying: "time heals all wounds" is true, but I don't like the wording of that phrase. That's not giving YOU the credit you deserve. Time isn't healing your wounds, life isn't getting easier because you're older... YOU are leveling up, YOU are healing your wounds, YOU are finding clarity.

It's time to give yourself more credit. What is one thing YOU have grown to embrace?

- Maybe you now find it easier to ask for what you want...

- Maybe you now aren't nearly as critical of yourself as you used to be...

- Maybe you now truly see rejection as redirection... YOU have grown.

YOU have gotten smarter. YOU have gotten hotter. YOU have gotten more mature. YOU have grown with your standards and boundaries and confidence. YOU went through those experiences. YOU opened your eyes. YOU grew up. YOU turned those scars into unbreakable new standards. YOU turned those experiences into lessons that empower you. YOU did that.

Time heals all wounds? Sure. But more accurately, YOU heal your own wounds over time. Getting older is a gift. But don't be like, "Nahhh, I'm just older now... that's why things have changed." That's not why. You've gotten to this point for a reason. You've overcome a lot for a reason. It's not an accident. It's not just because of time. It's because of YOU.

Reminder:

Ambition and high
standards look great on you.

You smell great, moms love
you, and the world is a better
place with you in it.

You should be proud of yourself
for how far you've come.

You're fun to be around and
your energy is contagious.

Your weird is the weird
the world needs.

I deserve:

because I:

One thing I'm looking forward to:

What's a big deal to you right now? Why is it so important to you? What actions are you taking that respect its importance?

Day 35/60

Time is too precious to live someone
else's definition of happiness and success.
You are too wise to reopen doors you've
already closed. You are too powerful to wait
on empty promises and empty people. You
are too ambitious to do something just
because "that's the way it's always been done."

I don't ever want to look back and regret:

What's bothering you/on your mind right now?

One thing you will NEVER accept, tolerate, or settle for:

What is your definition of "success?" What will it take for you to reach that definition? How will you know you've made it?

Day 36/60

Just because I've experienced
darkness doesn't mean I won't
sprinkle sunshine wherever I go.

One thing I have:

One thing I want:

I'm the kind of person who:

Who is someone you miss? Why do you miss that person? How did they used to make you feel? How can you reconnect with that person or find a more permanent reflection of the way they made you feel in someone new?

Don't believe everything you feel

"Honor your feelings but don't trust them." Have you heard that saying before? It's the best advice you can live by as you navigate the ups and downs of your emotional inner life.

Why don't we honor our feelings but question them BEFORE we decide to trust them? When we do, we'll realize that in the same way some people don't belong permanently in our lives... many of our feelings also do not. But we only realize that if we take time to pause and question them.

"Is this a feeling I should trust right away? Should I trust this feeling at face value? Or is this a temporary feeling that does not define me and doesn't belong in my house?" Give yourself the gift of pausing for a moment. What evidence do you have that this is a real and permanent feeling?

Hopefully when you address a feeling this way, you'll realize the feeling is a feeling because you've been feeling it. That's it. YOU get to decide what the facts are in your life. You get to decide if the feelings you face are allowed into your house. You get to decide if they are worthy of a seat at your table. The next time you get an incoming feeling, pause:

- you'll realize that you can feel anxious, but it doesn't mean you're falling behind.

- you can feel unworthy, but that's just because someone didn't see what you bring to the table. And that's their loss.

- you can feel like you're lost, but it doesn't mean you can't find your stride.

Feel what you feel, but don't trust it right away. That is a gift you deserve to give yourself.

****

It's time for you to bet on yourself.

It's time for you to be given the
spotlight you've always given others.

It's time for you to meet the
reason why you never settled.

It's time for you to see the moves
you've been making finally pay off.

REFLECT: one word to describe how you currently feel:

REINVENT: one word to describe how you want to feel:

REBEL: one thing you can do today that is the opposite of what you've been doing:

If I prioritized how my life looks to other people, I would:

If I prioritized how my life feels to me, I would:

Do you have a dream you've let go of in life? What changed in your life that led you to let go? What would re-approaching that dream look like to you today? What would have to change for you to give it another try?

Day 38/60

Never let someone convince you to hide
a side of yourself to win their approval.

Never let someone convince you to offer
them something they cannot reciprocate.

Never let someone convince you that their
love is conditional on you changing who you are.

Never let someone convince you that you're
overreacting when you're standing up for yourself.

What's the best that could happen in your life right now?

One thing I can control:

One thing I should accept:

What's a conversation you need to have and with whom?
Why have you been putting this conversation off? How
would it feel to finally have it? What freedom, healing, or
direction would it offer you?

Day 39/60

You should be proud of yourself…

… for trusting your own timeline
instead of borrowing someone else's.

… for being your real self in a world
that encourages you to just fit in.

… for holding onto a standard even
when it's easier to lower the bar.

… for not limiting your potential
based on a previous life chapter.

I deserve:

because I:

One thing I'm looking forward to:

What affirmation do you need to hear right now? Write it for yourself. Be specific. Give yourself the optimism or hope you need to hear right now:

The case for being a hot mess...

After a lifetime of trying to be perfect and wanting to surround myself with other perfect people, I've realized the importance of being whole, not perfect. To be whole is to be proud of yourself for trying, it's to surround yourself with other eager people who want to collect memories rather than regrets. Those are people who are willing to fail, start over, and try everything at least once. Some might call that being a "hot mess" and so be it! I love being around people who would rather be a "hot mess of happiness" than perfect.

Those are people who realize the beauty of life comes from boldness. Imperfection. Second chances. They make music or art simply because they want to. They pursue what makes them curious. They would rather hear "no" than wonder "what if?" They listen to other people's stories, learn new cultures, and taste new foods. They open their hearts and let new kinds of love in. They strive to be whole, not perfect.

Be unreasonable. Prove what you're made of. Ask for a raise. Say NO and mean it. Make the first move or care first. Reinvent yourself... again. Say HI to every dog you see. Speak your mind freely. Take a compliment at face value. Call someone (the horror!) instead of texting. Be upfront about what you want. Embrace both your masculine AND feminine sides. Go to dinner alone. Change your mind... again. Unfollow anyone who makes you feel less. Love your body as it is today. Stand up for yourself without saying "sorry." Stop asking for permission. Decide their labels don't define you. Show others how you expect to be treated. Make eye contact first. Book a solo trip. Remove "good enough" from your vocabulary. Decide your past doesn't dictate your future. Be unreasonable.

Day 40/60

****

Life gets better when you start seeing redirection as an upgrade. You have the audacity to give yourself what someone else wouldn't. You see people for who they are, not who you want them to be. You decide their limits do not limit you.

I don't ever want to look back and regret:

What's bothering you/on your mind right now?

One thing you will NEVER accept, tolerate, or settle for:

What is something you used to want but don't want anymore? What changed your mind? What do you now want in place of that thing?

Day 41/60

****

I owe it to myself to focus on ME.
No drama. No negativity. Just a life
filled with weird friends, unconditional
love, adventure, and peace.

One thing I have:

One thing I want:

I'm the kind of person who:

What's a specific problem you can identify in your life right now? How does it present itself and how does it make you feel? What's one specific solution you can consider to the problem? Pretend this was your friend's problem and you're giving them advice about it:

Day 42/60

I'm no longer attending every argument or drama I'm invited to. Instead, I'm focusing on what brings me joy.

REFLECT: one word to describe how you currently feel:

REINVENT: one word to describe how you want to feel:

REBEL: one thing you can do today that is the opposite of what you've been doing:

If I prioritized how my life looks to other people, I would:

If I prioritized how my life feels to me, I would:

How often do you do things with no goal in mind - aka joy for the sake of joy? When was the last time you did something just because you enjoyed it? How can you introduce more joy like this into your life?

Healing is transformation

When something happens in life that drains you... what do you do? Do you power through and hope it'll all make sense one day... or do you take time to heal?

Breakups. Personal loss. Rejection. Betrayal. Failure. Embarrassment. What do you do following those experiences? You need to heal. You need to transform.

Needing to heal doesn't mean you're soft, overly sensitive, or too emotional. Experiences don't just appear and disappear in life. They extend into our essence, values, and way of seeing life unless we address them.

Healing is transformation. Healing is the process of transforming one not so ideal thing into something that is much more redeeming. Healing isn't fixing something completely. Healing isn't closure. That will come. Healing is transformation.

Ask yourself... what can I transform it into?

Rejection can become pride.

Heartbreak can become a higher standard.

Disappointment can become resolve.

Take a minute and ask yourself that question... what do I need to heal from? And then transform it. A becomes B. Negative energy becomes positive energy. That is healing. One day, you'll look back and realize how that new transformative energy serves you and you'll be amazed by the closure you created for yourself.

Day 43/60

My love language is being
weird and seeing who it
scares off and who stays.

What's the best that could happen in your life right now?

One thing I can control:

One thing I should accept:

What's something that makes you feel small in life? Is it something that someone else controls or that you control? What about the opposite - what's something that makes you feel big or empowered?

Day 44/60

Life is so much simpler
when you stop listening
to people who tell you
to be "realistic."

I deserve:

because I:

One thing I'm looking forward to:

How can you simplify your life? What are some habits, people, or thoughts you have that you could do without and maybe are better off without? In what ways can you "unbecome" in order to become your boldest self?

Day 45/60

You should be proud of yourself
for keeping your heart open even
though your past taught you it's
safer to keep it closed.

You should be proud of yourself for
being a kind person but still showing
people how you expect to be treated.

You should be proud of yourself for
deciding your story is so much more
than the limits of its past chapters.

I don't ever want to look back and regret:

What's bothering you/on your mind right now?

One thing you will NEVER accept, tolerate, or settle for:

What are three things you're proud of yourself for in your life? Focus on the things you've overcome, the doubt that no longer exists as heavily as it used to, and the challenges you faced and evolved through. Write this three times:

I'm proud that I _____

I'm proud that I _____

I'm proud that I _____

Take your own advice

Are you that friend who gives great advice? Do you give top tier *chef's kiss* advice to your friends on their dating life, their career, etc.? BUT then when it comes to your own life, you don't take it? You resort to what you normally do. You resort to comfort. You resort to stubbornness. You resort to fitting in.

Why don't we take our own advice?

We use age as an excuse A LOT. "I can't change now. I've invested too much into this habit or this endeavor or this mindset or this timeline." We're VERY capable of learning to take our advice no matter how old we are or what stage of life we're in... we just need to think smaller.

To convince our stubborn human selves to take our own advice... we need to think small and not big. Take your own advice for 24 hours. That's it. See what happens. That is how we end up taking our own advice in the long run. Think smaller. Small moments show us that it's never too late. For 24 hours...

- Today I'm going to slow down and appreciate what I have.

- Today is the perfect moment to take one small step towards that thing I've always put off.

- Today I'm not going to compare myself at all.

- Today I'm going to compliment myself and be kind to ME.

Do that today. And then when you wake up tomorrow... take your own advice again. Eventually you'll look back and you'll be proud because you're finally taking your own advice.

****

I'm at a point in my life where
everything I've "lost" is being
replaced by something better.

"Good enough" is no longer
part of my vocabulary.

I'm no longer scared to ask
for more. I said what I said.

One thing I have:

One thing I want:

I'm the kind of person who:

What piece of advice would you give yourself five years ago?
Write it out fully based on what you know now:

Day 47/60

****

You are worthy of being loved
while you learn to love yourself.

You are worthy of the same love,
honesty, and intention you give to others.

REFLECT: one word to describe how you currently feel:

REINVENT: one word to describe how you want to feel:

REBEL: one thing you can do today that is the opposite of what you've been doing:

If I prioritized how my life looks to other people, I would:

If I prioritized how my life feels to me, I would:

Do you feel you are worthy of more? Be honest. Why or why not? What are the things you want more of? What would "more" look like to you?

****

The goal is to create a life
where you follow passion,
not expectation. You're an
unedited version of yourself
in a world begging for filters.

The goal is to create a life
where magic isn't something
you only believe in; it's
something you create.

What's the best that could happen in your life right now?

One thing I can control:

One thing I should accept:

What are three boundaries you refuse to negotiate in your life? Write each out and remind yourself why each is important to you and where the boundary comes from.

You're doing better than you think

You're doing better than you think. You're standing up for yourself. You're no longer desperate to quickly get over breakups, frustrations, betrayal, dishonesty, etc. That was the old you - always looking to get over those things, to find closure, and to heal quickly. Now you've recognized it's more important for you to move on from those things than it is for you to get over them.

You don't put so much pressure on yourself to get over those things TODAY. You've realized how important it is to move on instead of staying in one place revisiting the pain, the hurt, or the frustration from the past. You've also stopped running away from certain things in your life. You used to look to escape certain things. You'd run away from people who didn't treat you right, jobs that bored you, friends who never prioritized you, etc. But now you run towards the positive things you want and in doing so, you leave behind the rest. You're motivated to run towards instead of away. You've also realized that you don't FIND closure, you don't FIND love, you don't FIND purpose, you don't FIND confidence... you create it. You've put yourself in the driver's seat and:

- You're creating closure, not waiting to receive it.

- You're creating the relationship you want with the person you want... instead of hoping it just comes to you.

- You're working to find or create your dream job... not hoping your current job magically turns into it.

You've assembled the ingredients to the things you want in life, and instead of hoping they magically come together... you're DOING more and stepping out because you've realized that YOU create what you want in life. That is why you're doing better than you think.

Day 49/60

It's never too late to let go of baggage
that was never yours to carry.

It's never too late to see the good in
yourself that you always see in others.

It's never too late to reimburse yourself
for all the love and energy you've given others.

It's never too late to value consistency over
big words, loud compliments, or flashy purchases.

I deserve:

because I:

One thing I'm looking forward to:

What pain are you still carrying with you in life? Why does it still hurt? When does it hurt the most? Write it out and be specific about where it comes from. What is its origin story?

Day 50/60

Some people will overlook you.

Some people won't offer you the
same energy you offer them.

Maybe that's the sign you need
to commit to your story instead
of trying to fit in theirs?

Maybe it's time to be at a 12
when everyone else is at a 2?

Maybe it's time to realize you've
been given magic because you're
strong enough to claim it?

I don't ever want to look back and regret:

What's bothering you/on your mind right now?

One thing you will NEVER accept, tolerate, or settle for:

What are you better at than others? It can be small, silly, or something really specific. Does this skill make you proud? How can you capitalize on it in a bigger way?

Day 51/60

****

Life is short.

Dive headfirst into what
excites you. Go on that trip.
Love the people who matter to
you most. Eat the last slice.
Choose kindness over gossip.
Forgiveness over grudges.

Do what scares you. Be grateful
for all the blessings you have in
your life and create even more.

One thing I have:

One thing I want:

I'm the kind of person who:

What are five ways you are fortunate in life right now?

Closed mouths don't get fed

The next time you feel yourself shying away from speaking up for what you want in life, remember: you ALWAYS win when you speak your intention, ask for more, or seek out clarity. Every. Single. Time.

Reason being?

You either get what you want (yes! here's more) or you get what you need (no! denied) but now you're free to move on to another person, setting, company, etc. who can provide the "more" you want.

The result of speaking up is guaranteed to be one of those two scenarios. Make that your mantra when you find yourself shying away out of fear of being "too much" or fearing rejection.

"Get what I want or get what I need."
"Get what I want or get what I need."
"Get what I want or get what I need."

Get what you need or get what you want. Whatever happens, it always serves you. It either delivers the outcome you want, or it provides the clarity you need to move on. You're always winning when you speak up because you're not sitting in the land of ambiguity. You're not sitting in the gray hoping someone else gives you the clarity you want. If you want different, you need to move different, speak different, and ask for different.

Life gets better when you stop being subtle about what or who you want.

Day 52/60

Have you noticed how peaceful
life becomes when you let go of
"supposed to be" timing and
just trust your own?

REFLECT: one word to describe how you currently feel:

REINVENT: one word to describe how you want to feel:

REBEL: one thing you can do today that is the opposite of what you've been doing:

If I prioritized how my life looks to other people, I would:

If I prioritized how my life feels to me, I would:

Complete the following phrase five times:

I trust myself to _____

I trust myself to _____

I trust myself to _____

I trust myself to _____

I trust myself to _____

Day 53/60

If you've been overlooked but
refuse to overlook yourself...

If you've been through a lot
but refuse to let it turn you cold...

If you've finally decided "you deserve
better" is undeniably true...

If you ever walked away from something
that wasn't working for you...

... you deserve to be happy.

What's the best that could happen in your life right now?

One thing I can control:

One thing I should accept:

In what ways do you feel underestimated or overlooked n life? Do you underestimate yourself? Do others underestimate you? How can you turn this feeling into something that inspires action or perseverance?

Day 54/60

Have you ever been called "too much?"
Too ambitious? Too independent?
Too sensitive? Too difficult? Too bold?

Maybe you are and maybe that's
exactly who you're supposed to be?

Being "too much" is making music
or art simply because you feel compelled to.
It's pursuing what makes you curious. It's
replacing "maybe" with "definitely."
Feeding your soul. Listening to other
people's stories. It's learning new cultures
and tasting new foods. Introducing yourself.
Realizing that your dreams aren't as big or
unrealistic as you once thought. It's letting
new love in. It's opening your heart and
mind to new kinds of love.

Life can be messy but being "too much"
is what makes it a beautiful mess.

I deserve:

because I:

One thing I'm looking forward to:

What are three things you never want to change about
yourself? Why are those aspects of who you are important?
How does each enhance your life?

When you need to make a change

The number one reason we don't actually make the changes we need to in life is because we allow ourselves to think of change as risk. We're hardwired to be comfortable, to survive, and to not mix things up unnecessarily. We go into self-preservation mode. We close off. We tense up. We allow ourselves to overthink.

- I want to change my love for myself? That's a risk because I might seem too selfish! I might be throwing away good opportunities and good enough people, people who MIGHT make me happy. People who I MIGHT grow to love.

- I want to change my approach to my career? That's a risk because what if I find a new job and it sucks, and now I can't go back to that job that was ok?

- I want to date more compassionately and stop dating people who don't level me up? That's a risk because what if I get too picky and end up alone?

Not making a change is an even BIGGER risk. Staying in one place is a huge risk. Staying in the same pattern of behavior is a huge risk. Not loving yourself the way you're capable of is a huge risk. So, let's rethink this. Change is simply transition. And we're ok with transitions, right? Transitions simply lead us from one thing, one person, one circumstance to another. Rethink risk. It's not risk... it's transition and we need more transitions in life.... because that is where we find what we want and deserve.

Consider where you are today and where you want to be. What's in between? Transition. There's something much more inherently optimistic about relabeling change as transition. Know that there are optimistic outcomes and hopeful opportunities on the other side of those transitions.

Day 55/60

Mantra:

For my next chapter, I'm just gonna
be the funniest, hottest, and most
ambitious version of myself.

I'm letting go of "okay" in my life...
Okay relationships, okay sex,
okay compatibility.

I'm doing more of what makes
my soul happy and at peace...
even if I have to do it alone.

I don't ever want to look back and regret:

What's bothering you/on your mind right now?

One thing you will NEVER accept, tolerate, or settle for:

If you could say anything to someone who hurt you, what would you say and why? How would it feel to finally be honest about this to them?

Day 56/60
****

There's something beautiful
about someone who isn't
interested in fitting inside the
mold of what's expected of them.

One thing I have:

One thing I want:

I'm the kind of person who:

What is your definition of happiness? Be specific about the feeling and the actions that define it.

Day 57/60
****

How many moments are we saving
for a future day? A reason to wear
that outfit, say that thing, go to that
restaurant, or take that risk?

Stop waiting for "some day," for
the weekend, for the summer, or
for the perfect moment.

Take those shoes out of the box.
Buy yourself a cake. Pop champagne.
Plan that trip. Call your mom. Learn
a new language. Cook that dish. Say:
"I love you." Read that book.

Today is promised. Tomorrow is not.

REFLECT: one word to describe how you currently feel:

REINVENT: one word to describe how you want to feel:

REBEL: one thing you can do today that is the opposite of what you've been doing:

If I prioritized how my life looks to other people, I would:

If I prioritized how my life feels to me, I would:

Where has your head been most lately - past, present, or future? Why?

The power of laughing at yourself

Laughing at yourself means taking the pressure away you so naturally put on yourself. It means laughing at how serious you take your stumbles, how absurd your expectations are for yourself, how unrealistic your desire to be perfect is, how random life can be, and just how unlucky you can be sometimes. Laugh at yourself as often as you can.

- Before you jump to a conclusion of how much of a loser you are for losing a deal, laugh.

- Before you assume you'll never be some Rico Suave kinda character, laugh.

- Before you scold yourself for not saying the right thing or doing the right thing, laugh.

- Before you beat yourself up for forgetting something important, laugh.

Laugh at how inconsistent you can be sometimes. Laugh at yourself because you're being unrealistic. Laugh because you're not perfect and there's no need to expect yourself to be right now.

You know you're working on growing. You know you're working hard. You're putting in the hours. You're pushing yourself. You'll get there. But in the meantime, back off! When you feel yourself gearing up to doubt yourself, replace it with knee jerk laughter. Laughing at yourself trains you to love yourself before you doubt yourself. Laugh because you don't need to have everything figured out right now. Laugh because you're too hard on yourself. Laugh because you're human. Laugh because it heals you. Laugh because it makes you realize that you're really not lost.

Day 58/60
****

There's nothing wrong with
choosing what makes YOU happy.

You're cool with being alone but also
cool with falling in love. You're just
living your life but open to the day
when someone comes along and
amplifies the happiness you already have.

What's the best that could happen in your life right now?

One thing I can control:

One thing I should accept:

What's something you enjoy doing alone? How does it make you feel? How can you practice this more often?

Day 59/60
****

You'll be amazed by what you attract
when you refuse to wait around for
people who are unsure about you.

I deserve:

because I:

One thing I'm looking forward to:

What's something you refuse to give up on? Why is this thing important to you? Where does the motivation come from to keep going? Do you have an outcome in mind? What does that look like to you?

Day 60/60
****

I'd rather live with
the "oh wells" of
trying than the
"what ifs" of waiting.

I'd rather be a
hot mess living
life fully than
perfect playing it safe.

I'd rather have stories
of love and laughter than
memories of what might
have been.

I don't ever want to look back and regret:

What's bothering you/on your mind right now?

One thing you will NEVER accept, tolerate, or settle for:

Describe your "enemy" – aka the opposite of who you are. Write as many sentences as you can describing someone who represents all of the opposite values, ethics, and actions that you do. In the process, take time to appreciate what you represent and your discipline to stand firm in that person.

That's it. That's 60 days of cutting through the noise to become a bolder version of YOU. In the process of this, I hope you've realized that becoming MORE is actually about unbecoming.

Amidst all the things we complicate in life - taxes, relationships, our health, etc. - perhaps the most confusing one is the process of becoming ourselves. We try EVERYTHING to get it right. We try to find ourselves by emulating other people. We put more on our plate in an effort to find clarity through "trial and error." We strive for bigger goals, better bodies, and more perspective. That's all well-serving, but there's something to be said about simplifying the HOW of "finding yourself."

When Michelangelo commented on how he created the statue of David from a slab of stone, he said, "It's simple. I just removed everything that is NOT David."

With that comment, maybe Michelangelo was onto something bigger than just sculpture? Maybe the key to finding yourself is letting go of who you're not? Maybe finding yourself is less about becoming yourself and more about unbecoming? Consider that as you go about your week. What is something you can let go of that will allow the clarity you've already found in your life to shine through? In what ways can you "unbecome" in an effort to become? In what ways does a simpler but true life allow your boldness to shine?

- Case

* Want more? Listen to **New Mindset, Who Dis** twice a week on Mondays and Thursdays.

To listen on Apple Podcasts, scan below

Made in the USA
Las Vegas, NV
30 October 2023

79943516R00132